These Are My Senses

What Can I Smell?

Joanna Issa

Heinemann
LIBRARY
Chicago, Illinois

© 2015 Heinemann Library
an imprint of Capstone Global Library, LLC
Chicago, Illinois

Edited by Siân Smith
Designed by Richard Parker and Peggie Carley
Picture research by Tracy Cummins
Production by Victoria Fitzgerald
Originated by Capstone Global Library Ltd

Library of Congress Cataloging-in-Publication Data
Cataloging-in-publication information is on file with the Library of Congress.
ISBN 978-1-4846-0434-2 (paperback)
ISBN 978-1-4846-0447-2 (eBook PDF)

Image Credits
Getty Images: ArtMarie, 19, cover, Eric Audras, 9, Orbon Alija, 16, 20 (left), Stacey Newman, 5, 22 (right); Shutterstock: Africa Studio, 12, Eldred Lim, 8, Gelpi JM, 11, gosphotodesign, 13, Isantilli, 4, 21 (left), Julie DeGuia, 17, Mila Semenova, 15, Olga Lipatova, 18, 22 (left), back cover, Patricia Chumillas, 6, Roxana Bashyrova, 14, 20 (right), saisnaps, 7, Torsak Thammachote, 10, 21 (right)

Every effort has been made to contact copyright holders of material reproduced in this book. Any omissions will be rectified in subsequent printings if notice is given to the publisher.

Contents

What Can I Smell?

I smell cupcakes.

They smell **sweet**.

I smell rotten food.

It smells stinky.

I smell bread.

It smells yummy.

I smell dirty shoes.

They smell stinky.

I smell popcorn.

It smells yummy.

I smell flowers.

They smell sweet.

I smell a wet dog.

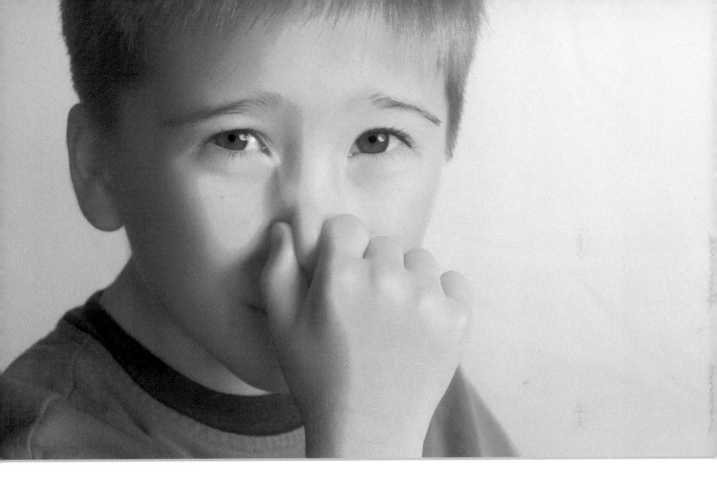

It smells stinky.

I smell soap.

It smells **fresh**.

Quiz: Spot the Difference

Which of these objects smells sweet?

Flowers and cupcakes smell sweet.
Wet dogs and dirty shoes smell stinky.

Picture Glossary

 **fresh**

 **sweet**

Index

Notes For Teachers and Parents

BEFORE READING

Building background:

Ask children about their favorite smell. Then ask children what smells are not so nice. How do children smell things? Do they think everyone likes the same smells?

AFTER READING

Recall and reflection:

What smells are from the kitchen? (cupcakes, bread)
What could they smell in the garden? (flowers)

Sentence knowledge:

Ask children to look at page 20. What kind of puncuation is used at the end of the sentence? Why is it there?

Word knowledge (phonics):

Encourage children to point at the word *smell* on page 5. Sound out the four phonemes in the word *s/m/e/l*. Ask the child to sound out each phoneme as they point at the letters and then blend the sounds together to make the word *smell*. Challenge them to say some words that begin with *sm*. (small, smart, smash, smart)

Word recognition:

Have children point at the word *stinky* on page 7.
Where else can they find the word in the book? (page 11)

EXTENDING IDEAS

Children might enjoy doing a "smell test" at home. Have them work with their parents to gather items to smell while blindfolded, such as onions, vinegar, bananas, and ginger. Can they identify the objects by smell? Which smells are their favorites?

In This Book

Topic

smell and senses

High-frequency words

a

I

it

they

Sentence stems

1. I smell _____.

2. They smell _____.

3. I _____ a _____.